Bits and Pieces Of Free Verse Poetry

By Elliot M. Rubin

Copyright May 2019
Library of Congress

ISBN 978-0-9981796-9-8

No part of this book may be reproduced in any form whatsoever without prior, express written consent of the author.

This book is fiction, and all names, people, places, and happenings are from the author's imagination and are used fictionally.

Any resemblance to any living or dead persons, and/or businesses, locations and/or events are coincidental in its entirety.

All rights reserved

Dedication
To my grandchildren
Shane, Isabelle, Jonathan, Carter,
Alexandra, Melanie, Mollie, and Madison

In Memory of
Herman S. Rubin
Who wrote poetry all his life.

Preface

Poetry is to be read and understood. To be written in plain English for everyone's enjoyment. Too often poets write in-depth, penetrating poems where you need to be well read and versed in the nuances of literature to fully appreciate the poem. Not this book, or any of my writing.
If you cannot understand what you read, then the poet failed; hopefully, I did not fail.

Other books of poetry by Elliot M. Rubin

Scrambled Poems from my Heart
A Boutique Bouquet of Poems and Stories
Rumblings of an Old Man
Surf Avenue Girl
Flash Pan Poetry
Unrequited Love
Aliyah - an Episodic Memoir
My Life if I took a Different Path - episodic poetry
Bent Twigs and Wet Feet
Stories of the South

Table of Contents

a song 6
alone 7
city streets 8
Dear Diary, ... 9
discovery 10
elegy for my country 11
gambling again 12
ghost wind 14
glass 15
glimpse from childhood 16
gone 17
high school untouchable 18
jelly donuts on display 19
Kindness & Love 20
leftovers 21
leftovers II 22
life cycle 23
lonely 24
love is in the air 25
madmen 26
mater lingua 28
my mortality 29
New York kismet 30
nightlife 31
one, a grammatical poem 32
Preordained 33

reality	34
suicide relief	35
summer camp hike	36
the small green bottle	39
time travel	40
tough girl	41
1951	42
A Shakespearian Sonnet from Brooklyn	44
writing	45
inner-city summer	46
a clean slate	49
going to the Ringling circus	50

a song

tonight,
as we hold hands
walking together
i feel your being
flow into my body

my heart pounds
with every step,
knowing
where we are going

the dance of love
brings you
closer to me,
as the music
plays
in my ear

i never knew
what a love song
meant,
until
my heart
met you

alone

i call out to him
"love you."
as my grandson
walks out of the room;
"you too" he calls back-
closing the front door

silence

the quiet reverberates
off the walls

sitting alone
in a darkened room
i remember holding an infant;
kissing him
till there was no feeling
left in my lips

now memories dance in my head

alone, i hear love
drive away
to find another
to kiss and hold tight

leaving me in silence

alone

city streets

the moon is low
street lights aglow,
i see ahead
men moving slow

flashes of fire
explosions
ring so loud,
straits are dire

guns dropped there,
they're running
everywhere,
bodies are down

dark windows
no one looks out,
they know better
it's not a lark

a drug deal went bad?
jealous lovers fight?
no one knows …
i'm safe i'm glad

Dear Diary,

i remember her as a newlywed
leaving the house, walking
to the farmer's field to pick wildflowers;
placing them in a clear glass vase
filled with water on the kitchen table

when she returned

the spring colors of light blue with
pale yellow petals, surrounded
by lavender florets and green leaves
brightening the start of every new day

decades later the farm is gone,
overgrown like weeds with new homes,
and she too has passed into memory,
leaving me with an empty vase

like my life is now

discovery

in the car
before
kissing
heavy breathing
glazed eyes,
moonbeams
on naked skin,
love began;
then she knew-
no longer virgin,
or heterosexual

elegy for my country

i mourn
the mighty imperial eagle
lying on the ground,
deadly talons
thrust in the air

once soaring high
amongst the clouds,
muscular wings
spread wide,
effortlessly
flying across miles
and miles

finally ending
as all empires do,
eaten by internal parasites
causing its demise

dead,
picked apart
by lowly animals
who once cowered
in fear

gambling again

the blackness
is all-enveloping,
my eyes are open
but i cannot see

elbows hit
a wall as
i try to move,
i can't sit up

lying flat
i fling arms
upward,
only to be denied
any movement

remembering
what the doctor
told me,
my loved ones
openly talking
about my funeral

am i dead?
buried?
gone?
underground?

an electric shock
prods me,
reverberating
through my body

light

brightness

deep breathes

i am alive
as EMT's
resuscitate me

i get to gamble
again
at the game of life

ghost wind

the barren
wheat field's
cut short,
harvested,
baled,
the combine
separates chaff
from seeds
spitting them out
onto a trailing truck

yet life continues
with the lone,
short daisy
standing tall;
its yellow petals
fluttering
in the ghost wind;
blowing invisible,
swaying the flower
back and forth
till planting
comes in Spring

when events
cut one down
and all is lost,
there is always
a ghost wind
to move you forward,
sometimes back,
but you are still there,
expecting tomorrow
to come again

glass

he walked out on her;
leaving a teenage marriage
of almost thirty years,
yet she was not upset

at work,
she smashed
glass ceilings,
working long hours,
playing hardball
with the boys upstairs

promotion after
promotion
till she reached
the top floor suite

the problem is
he loved her,
adored her;
yet could not
smash through the
glass wall she
placed between them

she outgrew him

glimpse from childhood

i don't know
why you ran
away,
nobody
was chasing
or wanting to
harm you;
except
in your mind

it's okay
to come back home

i forgive you-
for what,
i don't know?

looking forward to seeing
you in my dreams

i read
in the news
you are gone
for eternity

ghosted

we enjoyed
a long term romance
with vows of love-
i thought it's time
to get serious-
but you disappeared
from my life

vanished

ghosts
are invisible,
not seen
not found

no burial
no body
no prayers
only grief

you are gone
not forgotten,
a broken heart
is all that's left

high school untouchable

as she floated in the door
everyone stopped to stare,
not a hair out of place
her makeup so exquisite

i sat at a side desk,
she glided down the aisle
while staring straight ahead,
never looking at anyone in class

people were struck by her beauty,
i think she knew it too,
because she never looked down
while we all were looking up

right then and there i knew
i was untouchable.
i'd never be able to date her
or warrant a glance or two

until i became a lawyer-
when she came to me
for help in a divorce

i wasn't in her memory,
but she was always
in my dreams

jelly donuts on display

see them lined up
one after the other
soldiers at attention-
with powdered white sugar
coating their epaulets;
waiting to be picked

similar sizes all,
yet different,
a decision
is hard to make,
but i'll make one

filled with red jelly
round corners all,
fluffy yet firm,
i can taste them…
if i buy one

rest assured i will

Kindness & Love

The newborn is held close
To its mother, enveloped
In love, feeding to grow,
Feeling a soothing kindness
Stroking its small body,
Absorbing nutrients and
Antibodies to protect it

Years later,
On a deathbed
It lies still, sight gone,
Muscles atrophied,
Wrapped in blankets to
Keep warm, intravenous
Nutrients flowing into
Clogged veins-
Feeling the love
And kindness
From a caring
Hand
Gently rubbing aged skin,
While tears drip onto an
Uncovered arm,
Awaiting the Angle of Death

I firmly believe there are
Two basic rules in life…
Love and Kindness are to
Be ALWAYS given

leftovers

i always see people
order food,
then leave some
on their plates,
to be thrown away
at the end of the day

satiated
with a full tummy,
they think nothing
of leaving
leftovers,
instead of taking it home

in the heart
of Manhattan,
men
with empty stomachs
go dumpster diving
for restaurant leftovers
to eat

something is wrong
in a society of plenty,
when we can't
feed the hungry

leftovers II

i know she has
an explosive temper,
hurling expletives
and whatever else
was near her,
if upset

pretty beyond compare,
suitors by the dozen
lining up to court her,
till she becomes
volatile;
then they all walk
out,
leaving her
alone

a rare beauty
attracting men
like flies to wax paper,
no one sticks

we never dated

just hanging out
as friends;
until there were
no men left for her
to date…

except me

life cycle

after the new coat is worn
for years on end,
assaulted by harsh weather,
the tightly woven threads
spread,
succumbing to the closet,
never to be worn again

lonely

i never saw
a lonely flower,
they always grow
in bunches,
huddled together
sharing pollen,
helping
each other grow

no one is lonely
in a community
of love,
helping one another
in so many ways;
reaching out
to care,
this is how
it should be

hate and bias
go hand in hand,
destroying
a person's soul,
creating an outcast
loner personality,
unknowingly
killing themselves

people need people,
like flowers
gathered together

love is in the air

mothers hold babies
close to their chest,
embracing them
cherishing them
kissing them;
love is in the air

desiring a good life
for their children,
willing to sacrifice
as all mothers
want to do;
love is in the air

American
border guards
rip babies away
from brown-skinned mothers,
not white, cause
they aren't from Europe;
caged and separated
because of elected
white racists
in Washington, D.C.
love is not in the air

madmen

i have no issue with people
digging holes
in a field
before the sun
comes up,
sitting,
dressed in camo,
caressing
a rifle like a lover,
while earthworms and insects
look on
inspecting them,
their eventual meal,
as the hunter waits
for a flock or herd
to pass,
so something
can be culled
for sport or food

i do have an issue
with madmen
who enter
schools,
theatres,
social clubs,
or concerts
with military-style weapons,
to cull
children,
teenagers,
adults,
seniors;
for no rational reason

the question is
who are the real madmen?

the shooters?

or the politicians
who feed
at the breast of the gun lobby?

or the people
who continue to elect them?

mater lingua

i was born in this country-
English in my mother tongue,
Brooklynese is my
spoken language
of which I am quite fluent-
yet when talking, i do notice,
people crook their necks to listen;
cause i never diagram my sentences
mixing verbs, nouns, and subjects,
while ending with a proposition too-
grammar is not my strength,
or spelling for that matter either.
i use woids not found too often,
with accents not all comprehend.
so when you meet someone from
Brooklyn, just listen, you'll understand,
even when we talk with our hands,
or some of our fingers!

my mortality

a bushel of summers
have past
since i frolicked
in my youth,
believing in tomorrow,
because it's always coming

i never looked back
at the past
till the present,
now i don't see
many tomorrows
ahead

it is not the future
i fear
but the lack of it,
the self
lost,
forgotten,
like individual
grains of sand
mixed in with others
for eternity,
eventually
there will be
no i to remember

New York kismet

our eyes met
for a breaths
duration

then you're gone…

disappearing

walking up
the crowded
subway stairs

as my train
pulls out of
the station

nightlife

late night clubs
booze flowing smooth
girls at the bar
pretty as a flower

bees buzzing 'round,
pants full of pollen
looking for a petal
to pluck for the night

the choicest florets
always go first
leaving the weeds
for the rest of the hive

the sad truth is
a pretty bright petal
sometimes is bait
for a man-eating flower

floating 'round, the
butterflies swoop in,
sipping sweet nectar
bought by the bees

'til they get caught,
beautiful wings clipped,
innocence taken;
ending their night

one, a grammatical poem

almost all think
they come in pairs
when they hear
this spoken word

but it's singular,
by its lonely self,
all alone, hanging out
for all to see it's mark

there is only one
tittle in tittle,
so don't look for
two, it's not there

unknown till now
you too will see,
the dot on an i
is called a little tittle!

Preordained

sometimes

you can see the future

sometimes

you can't

sometimes

it just happens

sometimes

you can't deal with it

sometimes

you can

sometimes

it really doesn't matter

*can the future change
if we know it's coming?*

reality

he told me
there were things
he wanted
to buy
his two-year-old girl

a bike
a dollhouse
a dress for prom
a handheld mirror;
so many other things

today
twenty-five children
entered
the pediatric cancer floor,
only five walked out

his daughter was not one of them

grief, he said, *touches a heart*
like no other emotion…

who do you get mad at?

suicide relief

is suicide
a negative act?
ending the pain
is not a good thing?

your loss hurts those
who love you,
but does it bring
relief
from your demons
to others?

i don't know

summer camp hike

i remember
as a young camper
hiking
in Vermont
one hot, humid summer,
looking down
for tree roots
jutting out
from the ground

so i didn't trip

the higher we went
the cooler
the air became,
until we began
to chill
from slight breezes
evaporating
moisture on our
sweating bodies

the smell of nature
to a city boy
is refreshing

it isn't the smell of
pastrami or corned beef
wafting out
open doors
of a kosher deli
i inhale
as i pass

missing
is the odor
of hot poured asphalt,
or the rumble
of big trucks passing,
shaking the ground
as they dipped
into large
open potholes

for the first time,
when we stop
i hear birds chirping;
see a deer
in the distance
standing still,
staring at us,
before it scampered off
blending into the forest

camping
on the mountain
i was lying
near the campfire,
hoping
the flickering flames
would keep away
hungry bears

i fell asleep
from exhaustion
on hard mountain dirt,
in a sleeping bag
my cousin used,
years ago
when he was a camper;

but not before
the counselor
told us scary stories
of the severed,
murderous,
monkey's hand

those were exciting
days of my youth

the small green bottle

the smell of old age permeates
the room,
shades half up,
family pictures on the wall

i notice white doilies
on the club chair's arms,
blending in with her floral dress,
white hair, and the slipcovered
Sheraton sofa in the well-kept home

in her hand is a small green bottle
reflecting the morning sun's rays,
exposing the half-full liquid
which tastes like whiskey
when dabbed on my finger

asleep,
i silently watch her,
waiting to see her awake;
but the little green bottle
did its work so well

time travel

yesterday
i was seventeen
in high school,
surrounded
by teenage girls
flirting,
smiling,
dating,
enticing me

today
i am seventy-three
walking in a parking lot
to the supermarket,
surrounded
by white-haired
old ladies
barely seeing
over their
steering wheels

i feel like i traveled in time

where is my youth?

tough girl

hanging at the club
cycles parked out front
proudly wearing colors,
she goes inside fearless

guys drinking, gambling
some bitches joining in,
things go easy, guzzling
till someone spills on her

what the fuck you doin'
youse spilled it all on me
voices rise in anger
hands go in their pockets

space is cleared around as
knives flip out and open-
men back up to watch
while blood is soon to spill

one poke is all she needs-
he falls face down real hard,
a man runs up to lead her as
they roar away on bad-ass Harleys

later his luck runs out,
she cut his throat and ran,
cause only he knew her;
tough girl is gone forever

1951

i was six, placed in the front seat
of my father's Hudson Hornet, as he
drove the family to a working farm
for a summer away from the city;
with no air conditioning, my stomach
was turning, i felt nauseated,
carsick, nothing to do but try
not to throw-up

my cousin and i played
in the fallow pastures,
inhaling the sweet aroma
of cut grass mixing in
with the piles of cow dung
scattered about

Schmidt's Farm in Middletown
was next to the race track.
on weekend nights we watched
mini Offenhauser race cars
scramble 'round the dirt-floored oval

next to the main field was a small
pasture, wedged between the track
and a forest; with a narrow path
leading to a freshwater creek
holding a pond in a crook of the flow

fish, frogs and small snakes swam
with us, and mother brought a
blanket for picnics under the trees,
away from the slimy green moss
where we would dry off and eat

one summer ending, a
small feline was brought
to guard the barn.
i played with it, a tiny, friendly
pussy cat; harmless and furry

next year it stood guard
by the barn door
when i came back to the farm;
the cat became a lion,
not approachable, big and a
a stomach filled with rodents;
ending my last summer
on the farm.

A Shakespearian Sonnet from Brooklyn

If Shakespeare wrote sonnets in Brooklynese
Would Hamlet talk like tough guy Anthony
To many, deese woids sound like Taiwanese
And commit a crime like a felony?

Alas poor Ophelia lying in bed
When Hamlet finds out, still a virgin,
Crazy thoughts go through his youthful young head
Sadly, his eyes see a grounded sturgeon

Lady Macbeth loves cold New York water
Every chance she gets she drinks it a lot
For suckling child, a boy or a daughter
Or washing her clothes to get out damn spot

On Brighton Beach, many lovers do meet
Not this sorrowed group, no sand on their feet

writing

it is not easy to write
when autocorrect
corrects what it thinks
is correctable,
ignoring the intent
of a passage;
sending out incorrect
corrections
to make me seem
incoherent

this it does correctly!

inner-city summer

standing by the tall chain link fence
watching
young men play ball,
her eyes sight
one player in particular,
who is running around
scoring points

sweat is running down his chest
glistening
in the summer sun,
while the concrete court
radiates
intensive heat

July in the city
leaves jobless teens
little left to do
except play or make
mischief
in the neighborhood

unnoticed,
she leans
against the fence

when the game ends
the next group
waiting in the wings
walk on the court
ready to do battle
between the baskets,
trying to impress onlookers
standing by the fence

smiling at him
as he passes by,
she catches
his eye
causing him to stop
and start
a smart ass
conversation,
soon
they are walking
to his apartment house

his mother is upstairs,
so they go down rear steps
to the cold,
dry basement
to relax
get intimate

Too intimate for most

her hand glides
over gang tattoos
on his chest and arms,
ignoring signs
warning others
to stay away;
but it's too late for her

two days later,
the police dogs
find her body.

nobody
saw her leave with him,

not even one
of the hundred
watching the games

silence
is the city's code
when something bad goes down

no one gets involved

at her funeral
silence
rears its head again,
breaking through
her mother's tears

a clean slate

new school
new friends
new boys
starting over

long blond hair
ruby red lips
queen bee figure
tight blue jeans

sparkling blue eyes
softly spoken words
everything you'd want
to be seen with at school

this time she knows better,
to keep it to herself,
not to run about
no time to come out

she'll date a boy or two
it'll always be platonic
till she goes away to college
to be free enough to bloom

going to the Ringling circus

the tickets for the circus
were not too expensive,
the seats high up
on the lower level are good,
the flying trapeze artists
are at eye level,
i can see the fear
in their grinning face
as they release
from the brass bar

flipping in the air
with no net below,
they pass each other
with outstretched arms;
grabbing
onto the swinging bar
before it returns
to the other side,
riderless

the young woman
with her hair
up in a bun
wearing
a sequined costume,
looks so young
from afar,
but at eye level
the years in the air
took its toll
on her nerves,
showing in her eyes

pink cotton candy
sticks to my fingers
when I pull it
to my mouth,
licking them
to savor the
sweet taste again

the hawkers
walk up and down
the aisles
selling caramel popcorn,
ice cream,
sodas,
to the people
sitting and gawking

finally, clowns run out
causing mayhem
in the center ring:
red noses,
baggy pants,
a spritz of seltzer
to enthrall the crowd,
as a small car
drives in
spewing
more of them out

the elephants
come lumbering
in the tent,
as they enter
the center of the circus
to do their act

riding on top
of the lead animal
is a young girl
waving to us
as she passes
by my section

in my seventies,
i remember it well,
too well,
as the circus is no more-
it now only exists
in my memory;
my grandchildren
will never experience
my joy
under
the big top

www.ingramcontent.com/pod-product-compliance
Lightning Source LLC
Chambersburg PA
CBHW051718040426
42446CB00008B/945